J 537 MUR
Murray, Julie,
Electricity / by Julie
Murray.

D0929328

ELECTRICITY

FOUNTAINDALE PUBLIC LIBRARY DISTRICT
300 West Briarcliff Road
Bolingbrook, IL 60440-2894
(630) 759-2102

A Buddy Book

by

Julie Murray

ABDO
Publishing Company

VISIT US AT
www.abdopublishing.com

Published by ABDO Publishing Company, 4940 Viking Drive, Edina, Minnesota 55435.

Copyright © 2007 by Abdo Consulting Group, Inc. International copyrights reserved in all countries. No part of this book may be reproduced in any form without written permission from the publisher. Buddy Books™ is a trademark and logo of ABDO Publishing Company.

Printed in the United States.

Series Coordinator: Sarah Tieck
Contributing Editor: Michael P. Goecke
Graphic Design: Maria Hosley
Cover Photograph: Photos.com
Interior Photographs/Illustrations: Clipart.com, Fotosearch, Media Bakery, NASA, Photos.com

Library of Congress Cataloging-in-Publication Data

Murray, Julie, 1969–
    Electricity / Julie Murray.
      p. cm. — (First science)
    Includes bibliographical references and index.
    ISBN-13: 978-1-59679-822-9
    ISBN-10: 1-59679-822-X
    1. Electricity—Juvenile literature. I. Title. II. Series: Murray, Julie, 1969- First science.

QC527.2.M87 2007
537—dc22

                                  2006017154

TABLE OF CONTENTS

AN ELECTRIC WORLD

Electricity is part of our everyday life. It is easy to see electricity at work in many places. Just look around!

Electricity helps make sparks to start engines. It helps appliances, such as televisions, work. Also, electricity helps computers run.

Electricity helps make computers, kitchen appliances, and car engines work.

ELECTRICITY AND LIFE

Electricity helps make life possible. Along with magnetism, electricity creates a **force** that holds matter together. And, electrical **impulses** help make parts of the human body work.

The human body's electrical impulses help us to jump and move.

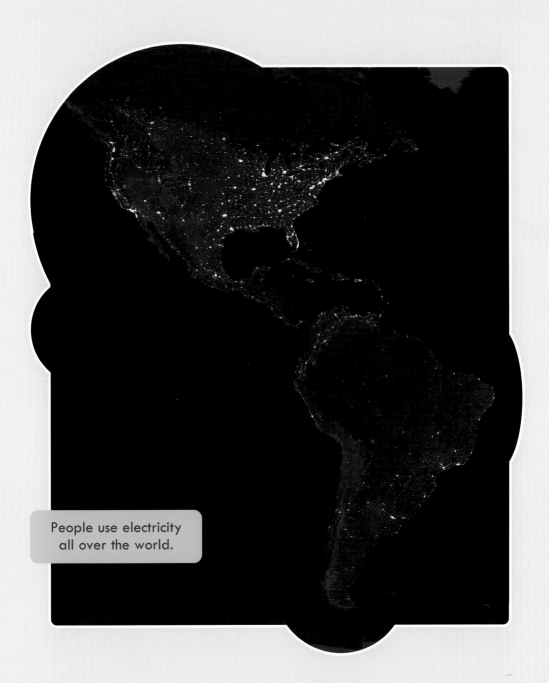

People use electricity all over the world.

THE SCIENCE OF ELECTRICITY

Electricity is a form of energy. The key to understanding electricity is knowing about matter, **atoms**, and charges.

Everything on Earth has matter. Anything that takes up space is matter. There are many different forms of matter.

Thumbtacks are made of matter.

All forms of matter are made up of **atoms**. Atoms are very tiny. But they are made up of three even smaller particles. These are protons, neutrons, and electrons.

Each atom has a **nucleus** at its center. The nucleus is made up of **protons** and **neutrons**. Protons have a positive charge. Neutrons have a neutral charge. **Electrons** swirl around the nucleus. Electrons have a negative charge.

The positively charged nucleus and the negatively charged electrons are **attracted** to each other. This helps hold atoms together.

The movement of positive and negative charges in an **atom** creates electricity. When the **electrons** spin around inside an atom, they create an electrical current.

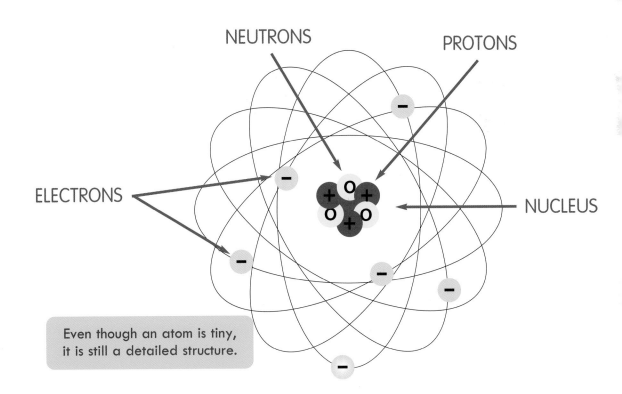

NEUTRONS

PROTONS

ELECTRONS

NUCLEUS

Even though an atom is tiny, it is still a detailed structure.

ELECTRICITY AND MAGNETISM

Magnetism happens because of the electric currents in **atoms**. When the **electrons** spin inside an atom they create both, an electric current and a magnetic field. This is called electromagnetism.

Electromagnetism is a very important part of the universe. This **force** is what holds atoms together. It is why all forms of matter exist.

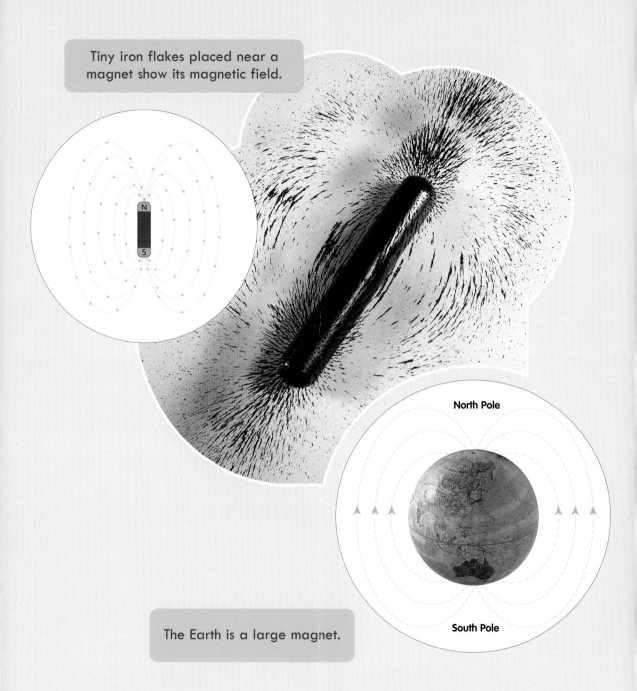

Tiny iron flakes placed near a magnet show its magnetic field.

North Pole

South Pole

The Earth is a large magnet.

Many years ago, homes didn't have electricity. So people used oil lamps and candles to make light.

In the late 1800s, American inventor Thomas Edison developed the lightbulb. The lightbulb used electricity to help people see in the dark. The lightbulb became an easier way for people to make light.

Today, most modern homes have electricity, and almost everyone uses lightbulbs. Lightbulbs come in many different sizes. They are used in flashlights, car headlights, and desk lamps.

Today, most people use lightbulbs in their homes.

CHARGING THROUGH HISTORY

Through the years, scientists have tried to understand how the science of electricity works.

Many years ago, it was discovered that some natural materials hold an electric charge. Since then scientists have done experiments and shared their ideas on electricity.

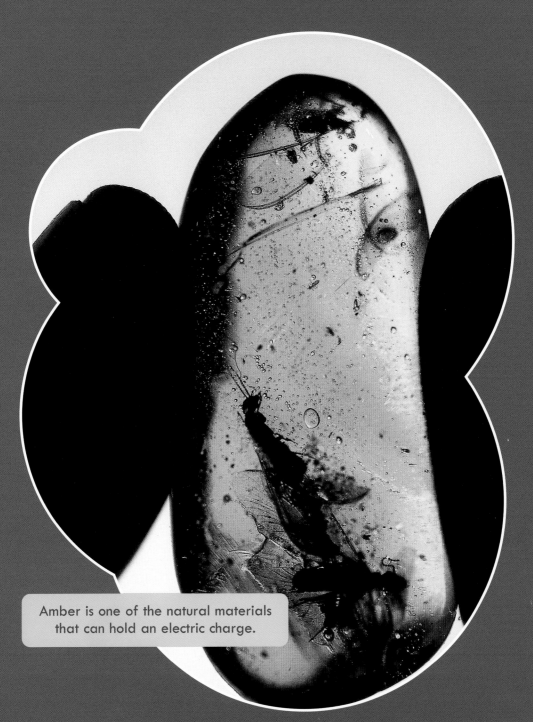

Amber is one of the natural materials that can hold an electric charge.

Benjamin Franklin is one of the most famous people to study electricity. In 1746, he began experimenting with electricity.

One of Franklin's most famous experiments involved flying a kite during a thunderstorm in 1752. He was trying to learn more about lightning's electrical charges. Today, people know this experiment was very dangerous.

Since these experiments long ago, many important discoveries have been made about electricity. Still, most people agree there is always more to learn about this science.

Benjamin Franklin wrote many important papers on his discoveries.

ELECTRICITY IN THE WORLD TODAY

Electricity helps people move through the world. Without electricity, many everyday objects wouldn't work. People would have to do the work that machines do. And, without electricity, lightbulbs wouldn't light up.

Machines use electricity to do many hard jobs.

The world would be a very different place if we did not have electricity.

Cities would be dark without electricity.

WEB SITES

To learn more about **Electricity**, visit ABDO Publishing Company on the World Wide Web. Web site links about **Electricity** are featured on our Book Links page. These links are routinely monitored and updated to provide the most current information available.

www.abdopublishing.com

IMPORTANT WORDS

atom a tiny particle that makes up matter.

attract to pull closer.

electron a particle in an atom with a negative charge.

force a push or pull against resistance.

impulse a sudden feeling that makes someone do something.

neutron a particle in an atom's nucleus with a neutral charge.

nucleus the center of an atom.

proton a particle in an atom's nucleus with a positive charge.

INDEX